SOCIALISTS AND WAR

TWO OPPOSING TRENDS

PSL PUBLICATIONS

SAN FRANCISCO

Library of Congress Control Number: 2012924237
ISBN: 978-0-9841220-6-6
Printed in the United States
Cover: Yang Guang, Xinhua
NATO bombing of Tripoli, Libya, June 7, 2011

Written by

Brian Becker, Mazda Majidi

Editor

Jane Cutter

Staff

Anne Gamboni, Nathalie Hrizi
Saul Kanowitz, Keith Pavlik

PSL Publications

2969 Mission Street #201
San Francisco, CA 94110
(415) 821-6171
books@PSLweb.org
www.PSLweb.org

Socialists and war: two opposing trends

1918	World War I ends, Middle East carved up by British and French empires.
1920	French troops overthrow newly-established Syrian state, begin colonial rule over Lebanon and Syria.
1940	Quick collapse of France at the start of World War II leads to the loss of control of the French colonies and the temporary British occupation of Lebanon and Syria.
1946	Syria achieves formal independence.
1949	First ever CIA-organized coup overthrows the government of Shukri al-Quwatli, installs short-lived right-wing government headed by Husni al-Zaim.
1963	Arab Socialist Ba'ath Party takes power in Syria. The Ba'ath Party, which also took power in Iraq the same year, had been founded in Syria in 1947. Under the motto of "Unity, Liberty, Socialism," Ba'athism represents a left bourgeois tendency of the Arab nationalist movement.
1966	The left wing of the Ba'ath under the leadership of Salah Jadid defeats rightist forces within the party. Jadid launches the widespread nationalization of industry and agriculture and extensive social programs to benefit the workers and peasants.
1967	Israel launches a lightning strike against its Arab neighbors in the Six Day War, defeats Egypt, Syria and Jordan; and conquers the West Bank, Gaza, the Sinai Peninsula and Syria's Golan Heights, which it occupies to this day.
1967-70	The Israeli military victory deals a heavy blow to the nationalist leaders of Syria and Egypt and weakens the more leftist and radical forces within both regimes. In Egypt, this leads to the ascension of a pro-imperialist regime after Nasser's death in 1970.
1970	Syrian military intervenes in Jordan in support of Palestine Liberation Organization but is driven back, with Israel threatening to intervene on side of Jordanian monarchy.

1971	Hafez al-Assad overthrows Jadid leadership.
1971-2000	Hafez al-Assad presidency. During his years in office, while maintaining a socialist program in name, Assad moves toward a more centrist, bourgeois-nationalist program. In foreign policy, Assad is inconsistent in taking anti-imperialist positions. Syrian security state forces use harsh tactics against political challenges.
1972	Syria signs defense treaty with the Soviet Union.
April 1976	Syrian army, with the backing of the United States, invades Lebanon during the Lebanese civil war, blocking the victory of the progressive forces led by the PLO and the Lebanese National Movement.
1982-2000	Syria supports Hezbollah and other movements resisting the Israeli occupation of Lebanon.
1990-91	Syria participates in the U.S.-organized coalition against Iraq in the first Gulf War. The Ba'ath Party had split years earlier and there was deep animosity between the Iraqi branch under Saddam Hussein and the Syrian branch under Assad.
2000	Lebanese resistance succeeds in expelling the Israelis from nearly all of the country's territory.
2000	Death of Hafez al-Assad; son Bashar al-Assad succeeds him as president.
2006	Syria supports Hezbollah and other movements resisting the Israeli bombing and invasion of Lebanon in 2006.
2008-present	Syria maintains good relations with revolutionary governments in Latin America, and these governments side with the Syrian state against the rebels in the current conflict.
March 2011	Anti-government demonstrations begin, evolving into armed struggle between opposition and government.

Since the breakup of the Ottoman Empire in 1918 following WWI and the division of the Middle East among the colonizing powers, states in the Middle East have been predominantly authoritarian and undemocratic in form. The British, French and U.S. imperialists installed right-wing, reactionary feudal elements to rule over most countries, the borders of which were determined on the basis of imperialist interests.

Even in countries that broke free from imperialist domination—such as Syria, Iraq, Libya and Iran—the ever-present threat of subversion, invasion and overthrow were not conducive to the expansion of democratic rights.

Contrary to propaganda about the U.S. promoting democracy and human rights, the most backward and repressive regimes have been U.S. client states such as Saudi Arabia, Qatar and Bahrain, where royal families rule. There is not even the pretense of elections or parliament.

In Qatar, 94% of workers—and virtually 100% of manual laborers—are migrants, denied all rights and subject to frequent abuse. In Saudi Arabia, women are not even allowed to drive cars. Yet, Qatar and Saudi Arabia are the two Arab states most involved in the coalition seeking the overthrow of the Syrian government, supposedly in the name of "democracy" and "human rights!"

While inconsistent in its policies, Syria remains an independent state, opposed to the domination of the United States and Israel in the region, generally allied with the socialist bloc, and thus is in the crosshairs of the United States. The state is the largest economic entity and the economy is not widely open to Western capital penetration. Several Palestinian organizations maintain offices in Damascus.

Introduction

THIS timely book deals with a sharp debate among organizations that consider themselves socialists.

Although embracing the label of socialists as a defining term of self-identification, the debate reveals that these organizations are actually on opposing sides in the war waged by the Pentagon and NATO to overthrow the independent governments in Libya and Syria. Moreover, the pivotal political differences go far beyond the immediate conflicts in Libya and Syria and speak volumes about the orientation of various "socialist" organizations to their "own" governments.

The pamphlet consists of three articles, two of which were previously published in the summer of 2012. Mazda Majidi's polemic, "When imperialist intervention 'goes wrong': cruise-missile socialists" was written in July 2012 and published in *Liberation* Newspaper and on the web site LiberationNews.org. Dan Glazebrook's interview with Brian Becker appeared under the title, "Libya and the Western left" and was published in the Dissident Voice on August 21, 2012. The article "Socialism and war: two historic trends" by Brian Becker is published here for the first time. The text of the original 1912 Basel Manifesto also appears as an appendix

Given that the wars waged by the United States and NATO are a dominant feature of the contemporary era, the issues addressed in this pamphlet could not be more important for those who seek to replace the current capitalist and imperialist world order with a new social system, one that is free from the scourge of militarism and endless war.

Cruise-missile socialists

When justifying imperialist intervention 'goes wrong'

BY MAZDA MAJIDI

ON July 1, an article titled "Libya and Syria: When Anti-Imperialism Goes Wrong" was published on the North Star website, signed by "Pham Binh of Occupy Wall Street, Class War Camp." The article argues that imperialist interventions in Libya and Syria are justified because they are demanded by forces the author calls revolutionary. While claiming to cut against the grain, he formulates what is a common position among liberals, progressives and even some self-proclaimed socialists and anti-imperialists. As such it is important to respond.

When imperialist countries intervene in the affairs of oppressed countries, the justifications do not only emanate from the U.S. government and the corporate media. In each instance, various forces and individuals with liberal and progressive credentials succumb to the imperialist propaganda campaign and put forth pro-intervention arguments, albeit using progressive-sounding analyses and using liberal or left language.

Even if "progressive" arguments for intervention originate far away from the halls of power, and do not receive a wide audience among the ruling class, they nonetheless play an important role in the imperialist war drives. This is because such arguments address a specific audience: people with anti-war and progressive inclinations who are typically far less susceptible to run-of-the-mill Washington and Wall Street pro-war propaganda. By spreading confusion about the nature of the intervention and the tasks of the progressive movement, those who would normally be the first responders in the anti-war movement are rendered inactive and passive. This is the value of this kind of propaganda for the ruling class.

In the lead-up to and immediate aftermath of each intervention, such forces emerge to explain that while anti-imperialism is good in general and in past scenarios, this time is different. Each time they present their arguments as new and unorthodox. While it is important to refute the specific arguments of the pro-intervention "left," we must begin with the broad observation that they continue a long and definite political trend in the imperialist countries. In the Iraq invasion, this trend received the name "cruise missile liberalism," but 100 years ago Lenin referred to it as "social-imperialism."

NOT ALL DEMONSTRATIONS AND
OPPOSITION MOVEMENTS PROGRESSIVE

The basic thrust of Binh's article is that the Western left must respect the wishes of the Syrian "revolutionaries" for foreign intervention. This, he claims, would constitute real solidarity and support for self-determination. In his entire article, Binh conveniently assumes the very thing that needs to be proven—that the Libyan rebels and the Syrian opposition are revolutionary. This false premise, once accepted, leads to all sorts of false conclusions.

What is the political character of the rebels in Libya led by the National Transitional Council? What qualified them as revolutionaries? How does Binh determine that the Syrian opposition is revolutionary and the government counterrevolutionary?

When analyzing an opposition movement anywhere in the world, this is the first question that needs to be asked. Just because part of the population of a given country comes to the streets or takes up arms does not mean that they are revolutionary or progressive. This is so even if they are responding to real social and political problems. Right-wing forces routinely mobilize parts of the population—predominantly disaffected elements of the somewhat privileged "middle class" and others—to promote right-wing agendas.

Fascists in Italy and Germany used rallies, marches and militant street actions as effective tactics to eventually take state power. In those cases, the fascists were not the opposition to socialist or otherwise revolutionary governments, but to bourgeois democratic governments that had been forced to grant some concessions to the working class.

In the United States, the Tea Party has staged rallies, including large ones of tens of thousands, in opposition to the Obama administration. No liberal, progressive or revolutionary would consider Tea Partiers to be revolutionaries.

In the aftermath of the overthrow of the Soviet Union, the U.S. government embarked upon a series of destabilization campaigns—often called "color revolutions." Most color revolutions occurred in the former Soviet Republics, such as Georgia's Rose Revolution, Ukraine's Orange Revolution and Kyrgyzstan's Tulip Revolution. But there have also been (successful or attempted) color revolutions in other countries, such as Lebanon's Cedar Revolution in 2005 and Iran's Green Revolution in 2009.

> *Just because part of the population of a given country comes to the streets or takes up arms does not mean that they are revolutionary or progressive.*

Color revolutions usually include the formation of coherent and unified pro-imperialist political forces, which draw upon public discontent with economic distress, corruption and political coercion. They involve several operations, including the creation of division and disunity in the military and an intense propaganda campaign. The extent to which color revolutions are successful is largely dependent on the level to which the targeted state is already destabilized by the time street protests take place.

Elements who participate in such street protests are often a small part of the population and do not represent the sentiments of the majority of the people, much less the interests of the working class. In fact, many participants in the protests may not support the agenda of the right-wing leadership and its imperialist sponsors. Still, the imperialist propaganda campaign utilizes the protests, however large or small, to promote regime change and the ascension of a client state. The imperialists are not fools to do so; this is precisely what such "democratic" movements produce absent an alternative working-class and anti-imperialist opposition.

Revolutionaries and progressives must stand on principles, and make a political assessment of movements in question. Even if the majority of the population were swept up by a reactionary movement, that movement is not revolutionary. Even if the majority of Libyans supported imperialist intervention—which is highly unlikely—that would not justify support by progressives for imperialist intervention.

Proponents of "humanitarian" intervention clearly do not suffer from a lack of analytical ability. What they lack is revolutionary resolve to stand up to an imperialist demonization campaign supported by all sectors of the ruling class.

WHAT IS THE POLITICAL CHARACTER OF THE SYRIAN AND LIBYAN REBELS?

The examples of color revolutions, fascist movements and right-wing mobilizations disprove conclusively the notion that demonstrators, dissidents and opposition forces are revolutionary by default. The Libyan National Transitional Council and the Syrian National Council fall in this category as well. These forces have staked their entire existence on imperialist patronage. Their statements in open support of imperialist intervention, capital penetration and "free" markets demonstrate the content of their vision, as does their prioritizing of diplomatic relations with the United States and its allies, including the potential normalization of relations with Israel. They leave little doubt about their political and class orientation.

What occurred in Libya, prior to the NATO bombing campaign, had the elements of a neoliberal color revolution, while also drawing upon the traditional fault lines of Libyan society (most significantly, regional competition from the oil-rich east as well as a long-standing trend of Islamic fundamentalism).

In the early stages, the revolt included street protests in Benghazi, the defection of some high-ranking political and military officials (from the government's neoliberal faction) to the side of the rebels and the formation of the pro-imperialist National Transitional Council. Immediately after the rebels took control in Benghazi, numerous dark-skinned Libyans and migrant sub-Saharan African workers were lynched in city streets in a wide-scale campaign of terror. Known supporters of Muammar Gaddafi's leadership were summarily executed; for months their bodies were found in ditches in and around Benghazi.

Despite a few initial victories, this rebellion lacked the strength to overthrow the Libyan government on its own, hence the necessity for foreign military intervention.

The NTC invited Senator John McCain, R-Ariz., to the "liberated" area of east Libya, giving him a hero's welcome. In a country that had long projected enmity, or an unstable relationship with imperialism, the rebels put up a huge billboard that read: "USA: You have a new ally in North Africa." NTC leaders traveled extensively through the capitals of Europe convincingly promising Western powers that their oil companies would have unrestricted access to Libya's oil. The message was: If we take over, there will be no more of Gaddafi's "economic nationalism."

U.S. LEFTISTS ADOPT CONFUSED SLOGANS

What kind of revolutionaries, while quickly earning a reputation for racist violence, would give away their country's resources to imperialist powers and beg them to bomb their country? In the face of these incontrovertible facts, some on the left, anxious to demonstrate their solidarity with the "revolution," falsely dismissed the NTC as merely a "clique" among a diverse and loose opposition movement. Clouded by their blind hatred for Gaddafi, and bending to the imperialist propaganda, they continued to describe the revolt as a "people's" or "democratic revolution."

While Binh writes that the left has been crippled by "knee-jerk anti-imperialism" with respect to Libya and now Syria, we observe the opposite. With few exceptions, the left failed to mobilize against the imperialist attack and regime change in Libya, and appears to be heading in the same direction with Syria. Accepting uncritically the "Arab Spring" label and the stories of impending humanitarian catastrophe, even those who claimed to oppose intervention did very little in practice.

Groups like the International Socialist Organization promoted the contradictory and academic slogan of "Yes to the Revolution, No to Intervention," which only spread confusion in the anti-war movement. After all, the Libyan "revolution" was the loudest champion of intervention. Its fate, whether it succeeded or failed, was based on the relative successes of the intervention. All the actors in the Libya conflict (the government, the masses who rallied against intervention, the rebels and the imperialists) understood very quickly that the "revolution" and the intervention had become indissolubly linked. The only ones who denied this reality were groups like the ISO, which believed they could magically separate the two with a rhetorical contrivance.

As the imperialists bombed away, the ISO ignored the masses of Libyans who rallied in defense of national sovereignty against imperialism, since they did not fit the convenient schema, invented by imperialist media outlets, of the "people versus the dictator." In practice, instead of joining a united front with all those standing up against intervention, they formed an anti-Gaddafi united front with Libyans in exile who championed intervention.

In a recent article, the ISO distinguished their position from the pro-intervention arguments of Binh. But their centrism paved the way for such social-imperialism (socialist in name, imperialist in practice). They accept all the same premises: that the Libyan government had no significant base of support and that the revolt was a popular "revolution" with an "understandable" desire for foreign help.

Moreover, the ISO pioneered the attack on "knee-jerk anti-imperialists" like the Party for Socialism and Liberation, leading the charge against us precisely as the war drums began to beat late last February. While misleading their readers that the United States and Britian "really, really do not want Qadaffi to fall" (Feb. 24, 2011) and downplaying the growing evidence of racist lynchings committed by the rebels, they lashed out dishonestly against anti-imperialists like the PSL.

Even when the bombing had begun, they repeatedly attacked the few anti-war forces taking action around Libya—for having caused a "wedge" with the Libyan "solidarity activists" who urged war. What is an anti-war movement for, if not to cause "wedges" with precisely such pro-war forces?

The ISO is now attempting to portray themselves as steadfast organizers against intervention, rather than offering self-criticism or reflecting on their own confusions and inactivity during the assault on Libya. Even now, when the rebel movement's right-wing political character has been made clear, they still attack the PSL for not supporting the "revolution."

Social-imperialists like Binh take the ISO's senseless centrist position a big step to the right, with a full-throated call to stand behind the NTC and imperialism. He instructs us to accept as a matter of faith that because the Libyan rebels were revolutionary, the NATO bombing was a revolutionary act and the opposition to it "counterrevolutionary"! Binh is not alone as a "leftist" in support of imperialist intervention; Solidarity, a non-Leninist organization that comes out of a similar political tradition as the ISO, published two opposing pro-intervention and anti-intervention positions on Libya.

A HIJACKED REVOLUTION?

Binh writes: "When the going got tough and the F-16s got going over Libya, the revolution's fair-weather friends in the West disowned it, claiming it had been hijacked by NATO." Some progressive forces first sided with the rebels erroneously, but knew better than to support the NATO bombing. The "hijacked by NATO" position was a way for such forces to gracefully correct their error and rhetorically oppose, or at least not support, imperialist intervention.

But not every political force in the West started out defending the Benghazi rebels. From the very start, the PSL was among a small minority that insisted on analyzing the political character of the opposition, pointing out the nationalist and contradictory elements of the Libyan state and exposing the imperialist motivations for intervention. Shortly thereafter, as more facts came out of Libya, the PSL and a few others exposed the right-wing character of the opposition movement.

The Libyan rebels were not a revolutionary force that was "hijacked by NATO." Irrespective of the motivations of individual protesters or rebels, as a political movement defined by its deeds, policies and strategic alliances, the counterrevolutionary thrust of the opposition movement was made quickly apparent. The NTC was a right-wing force even before it served as the ground forces of the NATO invaders. It utilized discontent among parts of the population, much of it with a regional basis, to reverse the remaining elements of the nationalist process initiated by the 1969 progressive coup, also called the Al-Fateh Revolution, led by Gaddafi.

Those who assert the NTC was an unrepresentative clique must face the fact that no progressive leadership ever broke from it, which presumably would happen if a progressive movement were openly "hijacked" by counterrevolutionaries! Nor did any rebels protest the bombing of their country. Even with the inevitable grumblings of discontent or dissent within the opposition rank-and-file against the NTC, this did not change one bit the overall trajectory of the movement towards counterrevolution.

POPULAR SUPPORT FOR LIBYAN REBELS?

Binh writes: "NATO's air campaign had mass support among revolutionary Libyans." Nearly unanimous popular support for the opposition is another unproven assumption of apologists for imperialist intervention in Libya, as well as Syria. The NTC did not enjoy the support of the entire Libyan population—nor does the SNC enjoy the support of the entire Syrian population. There is overwhelming evidence refuting such claims. On July 1, 2011, in the midst of the massive NATO bombing, hundreds of thousands—perhaps as many as a million people—rallied in Tripoli against NATO. The corporate media gave the protest scant coverage. Demonstrations of this size in a country of only six million people smashes the myth that the opposition had the support of all the people.

It is an uncontroversial fact that Libya, under Gaddafi's leadership, had a very small, almost negligible, military. After the NATO bombing started, the Libyan leadership opened up arms depots in Tripoli to the population, urging everyone to defend the country against foreign attackers. This is clear proof that, at least in Tripoli, the government enjoyed considerable popularity. Otherwise, why would an "unpopular dictator" arm the masses that would likely use the arms to fight against the state?

Binh suggests that the rebels were the key actors in overthrowing Gaddafi. But when, at the insistence of imperialist powers, the United Nations Security Council Resolution 1973 was adopted on March 17, 2011, the Libyan rebels were on the verge of complete defeat. Forces loyal to Gaddafi had been gaining control and rapidly moving towards Benghazi, having already made it past Brega. All of these are established facts acknowledged even by the pro-war imperialist media.

In fact, the rebels' imminent collapse was the reason the United States and its junior partners frantically rushed the resolution past the Security Council. If NATO had not started its merciless bombing campaign, the rebels would have lost all their remaining territory.

NATO carried out thousands of bombings and sorties over the course of seven months, delivering blows too severe for the Libyan state to overcome. NATO did not take its leadership from a ragtag group of NTC rebels that NATO itself saved from annihilation. On the contrary, during the months of the bombing campaign, the Libyan

Millions of Libyans protested NATO bombings, dispelling imperialism's portrayal of the struggle as Qaddafi v. the people.

rebels did not just receive military training and advice, but functioned under the operational command of NATO. In a coordinated fashion, NATO provided aerial support—that is, murdering pro-Gaddafi forces by bombing—which cleared the way for the rebels to move on the ground. The final siege of Tripoli was planned and operated by U.S. and European Special Forces units. Is this not evidence that the imperialist powers, not the NTC rebels, were in control?

Binh even praises "NTC's stand against foreign invasion and for foreign airstrikes." While NATO did not deploy ground troops in its military campaign in Libya, this was not due to NATO's respect for the wishes of the Libyan rebels. To the extent possible, imperialists always attempt to minimize their casualties by using part of the population of the country they are invading, occupying or bombing to do the fighting on their behalf. This is what Nixon's "Vietnamization policy" was designed to achieve.

The author correctly refers to the occupations of Afghanistan and Iraq as "transparent empire-building exercises." Yet, the United States did not land forces on Afghan soil until after the Taliban forces were already defeated by a combination of heavy U.S. bombardment and the U.S.-supported "Northern Alliance" Afghan forces on the ground. The preferences of the NTC in the case of Libya, or the Northern Alliance in the case of Afghanistan, were insignificant to imperialist plans. Imperialists want to minimize casualties, not because they care about the loss of life of their military personnel but to minimize the possibility of the growth of the anti-war movement at home.

In his zeal to attack anti-imperialists, Binh offers another apology for the NATO bombing campaign: "NATO's methods and the war's outcome were totally at odds with what the anti-interventionists envisioned: There was no massive NATO bombardment of civilian targets, there was no Libyan highway of death, no Black Hawk Down, no Wikileaks-style helicopter gunship atrocities." While accurate information is hard to come by, it is difficult to imagine 10,000 bombings in a country of 6 million did not cause wide-scale civilian casualties. The pictures of the destroyed city of Sirte are worth a thousand more words than Binh's reassurances.

THE MEANING OF SELF-DETERMINATION

Some assume that civilian casualties, inevitable in all such bombing campaigns, are the only or the main reason why anti-imperialists oppose intervention. Even if not a single civilian were killed in a given imperialist bombing campaign, (a virtual impossibility), it is still unjust.

Revolutionaries and progressives must not only stand with civilians, but recognize the ultimate justice of those fighting for their country's independence against imperialist attackers. The crowds in support of the Libyan government swelled once the imperialist bombing began, a testament to their sense of national dignity. They did not deserve to die. But in Binh's mind, those Libyans who risked and lost their lives to defend their country's independence against NATO and the rebels under their command were fair game.

Binh writes: "The moment the Syrian and Libyan revolutions demanded imperialist airstrikes and arms to neutralize the military advantage enjoyed by governments over revolutionary peoples, anti-interventionism became counterrevolutionary because it meant opposing aid to the revolution." According to this bizarre rationale, the right of self-determination, a right all progressives uphold at

NATO air strikes that left the city of Sirte in rubble illustrate the consequences of imperialist "humanitarian" aid.

least in words, means nothing less than support for imperialist military intervention.

In the imperialist era, the right to self-determination has been bound together with the "national-colonial question," that is, the specific global division of power between imperialist oppressor and oppressed nations. This has long been a cardinal question for revolutionaries inside the imperialist countries: What attitude will they take towards their own ruling class's imperialist plans, and towards the independence movements among the oppressed nations? Lenin, the Russian Revolution and the early Communist International recognized that these independence movements weakened imperialism and could hasten its downfall. They offered a united front, although not necessarily political support, to independence movements in the struggle against imperialism. This is the specific meaning of self-determination in the era of imperialism.

Regardless of one's political differences with or opposition to the Libyan government, those carrying the green flag became an independence movement when the imperialists started providing material support for the rebels, and eventually attacked.

IMPERIALISM IS A SYSTEM

Binh makes no attempt to explain why, in the case of Libya and Syria, imperialist powers happen to be on the "good side." Why would the imperialists unanimously support, not just diplomatically but militarily, genuine revolutionary movements?

Apparently, for those like Binh, imperialism is just a bad policy choice that can be reversed by good ones. In reality, it is a system that seeks world domination in order to secure its control of markets and capture of resources. It pursues the overthrow of independent states, even ones that only partly block the penetration and profit realization of oil giants and other profit-seeking corporations. This pursuit of markets and resources is the motivation for a rational and murderous set of policies, not subject to fundamental change by this or that politician, or this or that set of circumstances.

> *Why would the imperialists unanimously support, not just diplomatically but militarily, genuine revolutionary movements?*

Real anti-imperialists oppose all tactics imperialism uses to subjugate oppressed peoples, whether they are outright invasions, occupations and bombings or sanctions, coups, assassinations, funding and organizing pro-imperialist opposition forces, and propaganda campaigns.

It is possible for one imperialist country, or a grouping of imperialist countries, to temporarily aid independence movements in the oppressed world in order to weaken the hold of their imperialist rivals in a different country. This happened on occasion prior to World War II, when different imperialist powers were engaged in an intense struggle to expand their spheres of influence at the expense of others. At the end of WWII, U.S. imperialism became the dominant imperialist force. The other imperialist countries, both the victors and the defeated, were relegated to the role of junior partners to U.S. imperialism. In today's U.S.-dominated imperialist world, it is highly unlikely that one imperialist power will support a genuine revolutionary movement. It would be impossible for all imperialist powers to support and fund a genuine revolutionary movement. It would defy the logic of the imperialist system to do so.

The case of Libya was not about inter-imperialist competition, with one power supporting a liberation movement in hopes of making gains against their rivals. All the imperialist powers supported the rebels and have already benefited from the ascension of a client state. Hugely profitable oil contracts have already been signed, and are continuing to be granted by the generosity of the new Libyan government towards the oil giants. U.S. oil companies ConocoPhillips, Marathon and Hess Energy, France's Total, Italy's Eni, British Petroleum and other oil giants are each grabbing part of the spoils. The Libyan neoliberals, who had to compete with the nationalist-oriented forces inside the previous Libyan government, are firmly in control.

Binh considers what happened in Libya "a step forward," overlooking the racist lynchings and the wholesale betrayal of the Libyan nation to imperialism.

STANDING AGAINST IMPERIALIST DEMONIZATION IS NOT EASY

In its essence, this is not a theoretical issue. Binh and other proponents of "humanitarian" intervention clearly do not suffer from a lack of analytical ability. What they lack is the revolutionary resolve to stand up to an imperialist demonization campaign that all sectors of the ruling class supported. By comparison, siding with imperialist intervention is the easy thing to do; it is the path of least resistance to make a more "mainstream" and "respectable" left.

Binh correctly condemns U.S. interventions in Somalia, Haiti and the Balkans, as well as the occupations of Afghanistan and Iraq. But anyone can oppose past imperialist interventions as questions of academic and historical debate. When those interventions do not go well, even some ruling class politicians are critical.

The Binhs of the future will undoubtedly look back and condemn the Libya intervention as a historic crime, only to justify the next imperialist intervention. Revolutionaries, anti-imperialist by definition, struggle against imperialist interventions, not just in historical perspective, but more critically, in the here and now. □

Socialists and war: two opposing trends

BY BRIAN BECKER

MAZDA Majidi's polemic against Pham Binh and the International Socialist Organization was written about the conflict in Syria and Libya but its central arguments have a certain universal application and thus relevance for understanding the dynamics of contemporary wars, particularly those that pit the imperialist powers against governments that have been targeted for overthrow by the Pentagon and the CIA.

The article is important because the phenomenon of some socialist organizations supporting the same side as their "own" imperialist government, at a time of war, has emerged over the past century as a hallmark of the era.

In this case, Binh and the ISO are on the same side in that they desire the same outcome in the current war that aims to smash the government in Syria. But they have constructed two distinct lines of argument in defense of their position on how the Syrian "revolutionaries" should win their fight.

Binh argues that the Syrian "revolutionaries," like their counterparts in Libya, cannot win without imperialist military intervention and that NATO and Pentagon should do whatever it takes to get the job done. His argument is at least coherent, especially in contrast to the ISO position: There is no question that the Syrian government had and has the military capacity to defeat the "revolutionaries." The foreign assistance provided by the United States, other NATO powers and their regional allies like the Saudi royal family, has been crucial to the survival of the Free Syrian Army and the armed opposition to the Syrian government.

The ISO's position, on the contrary, lacks any internal logic or coherence in its application to the real world of war. It is useful in coffee shop discussions or at the group's chapter meetings where it will go unopposed. It takes dilettantism to a new level. The ISO argues that the Syrian "revolutionaries" should oppose imperialist military assistance and intervention even though it is precisely the aid and support from imperialism and the Saudi military that has allowed them to survive as a rebel army.

Majidi addresses the most pertinent question. What is it about the armed "revolutionaries" in Syria that makes their cause the rallying cry not only for the ISO but for all the imperialist powers and reactionaries, including the former colonizers of the Middle East and Syria? What is it about the political and social character of the two sides of the war in Syria that have created the real-life alignment whereby all the imperialist powers, without exception, support the cause of the Syrian "revolutionaries" in the war against the Syrian government?

One might argue that in the case of Syria, while the Pentagon and the CIA has helped the "revolutionaries" with money, logistical support, weapons transfers, a media propaganda campaign and economic sanctions against Syria; the United States has refrained so far from direct military actions and bombings such as it carried out against Libya in 2011.

That argument is without foundation. Even the seemingly least violent methods imposed by the imperialist powers against Syria are an act of war. Economic sanctions, financial aid to the rebel forces and weapons transfers are all parts of a war effort. Economic sanctions—often touted by some liberal groups as an alternative to war—are a method of devastating warfare by the powerful capitalist countries against the developing countries.

Economic sanctions imposed on Iraq in the 1990's took the lives of about 5,000 children per month, almost equal to the number U.S. troops who died in Iraq over the entire course of the nine-year occupation.

The United States and NATO powers are at war against Syria. That is the reality and that is the context for Majidi's polemic. The war is presented in the western media and by the NATO governments as a struggle between "the Assad dictatorship and the Syrian people." This is the same propaganda paradigm that is utilized by the ISO and Pham Binh.

This pro-imperialist mantra is not an accurate analysis of the complexity of the Syrian political and social scene. It is superficial and simplistic at best and a pinkish, i.e. semi-socialist, version of the imperialist demonization campaign at worst. In fact, it is both. This characterization of the war in Syria is both factually wrong and an accommodation to the prevailing media-driven campaign that is in full operation whenever the imperialists target a government for destruction.

Given that the Baathist government has pursued a strong secular policy, it should come as no surprise that it enjoys a wide base of popular support from some sectors of the population and is hated by others.

Twelve years of U.S.-backed sanctions were directly responsible for the death of over 500,000 Iraqi children

IMPERIALISM AND THE SYRIAN CIVIL WAR

The imperialist powers and their Saudi proxies are working with and through the Syrian armed opposition which they helped shape into an army. As in any class society, the opponents of the Syrian government are not a monolith. They have a wide range of grievances with the regime, including religious or ethno-sectarian issues along with political and social differences. Even among those who are defending the regime there are many who oppose this or that feature of the government. There was an organized section of the political opposition which wanted a reformed or completely different government, but opposed foreign intervention and armed struggle, i.e., civil war. This section of the political opposition to the Assad government was largely swept aside by the imperialists and their "revolutionary" allies in their pursuit of the tactic of civil war. The axis of the struggle is between the foreign-backed armed opposition and the Syrian government.

The United States, which is the dominant force in the Middle East today along with its partners, France and Britain, two former colonial enslavers of the Middle East, do not really care about "reform" or creating a "democratic" government in Syria. The form of government is of vital importance to the Syrian people but it has absolutely zero impact on the decision-making and calculations of the imperialists. Before independence the Western powers insisted that Syria be barred from self-government, much less "democracy."

Today, the main goal of U.S. and French imperialism is the creation of a new, dependent client regime in Syria. If they cannot end up with a stable puppet regime, the minimum objective is to have weakened Syria to such an extent that any future regime will be incapable of functioning as an independent power in this oil-rich region. In the last decade, imperialism has waged wars against Iraq and Libya, governments with a secular and nationalist outlook. These wars served as a wrecking ball of sorts, such that the destruction of core infrastructure was so great that both countries will be severely weakened for decades.

The notion, promoted by the Arab League, that the Saudi monarchy is sending weapons to the armed opposition because the Saudi royal family seeks democracy and human rights in Syria is so absurd that it is hard to envision how any journalist, much less a progressive one, covering this story would not endlessly expose this obvious contradiction.

SOCIALISTS AND WAR: TWO OPPOSING TRENDS

For nearly a century now, a section of the socialist movement inside of the imperialist countries has ended up on the same side as "their" government as it pursues war against its enemies. This is a universally repeated pattern and has happened in every imperialist war in the 20th century and continues today.

Sometimes these "socialists" openly and publicly embrace outright imperialist war and military intervention by their government. This is the case for the position of Binh when he unapologetically supports the NATO bombing of Libya and hopes for a similar plan for Syria.

Another "socialist" tendency, however, supports the primary objective of the imperialist government's war effort—in the present case the destruction of the Libyan and Syrian government—but differs with "their" government's tactics and avails itself of socialist rhetoric and socialist arguments to explain that their motives are far different and opposed to the imperialists who are conducting the war.

At the time of war these two currents of socialism—the right-wing socialists who outright support the imperialist war and the centrists who share the objectives of imperialism but take issue with the methods and motivations of those conducting the war—are part of the same political family. Their difference is like a spat between siblings. However much they may seem to disagree, no matter how heated the expression of their differences, they are bound together. What unites them is deeper than what separates them. They share the same goal. They want the same thing. The objective is fundamental. Their common objective, in the case of both the Libyan and Syrian war, is also the same as "their own" imperialist government.

Again, Majidi's polemic against these two currents of socialism is useful beyond the immediate issue of Libya and Syria because this political phenomena, whereby a section of the socialist movement inside the imperialist country ends up supporting—to one degree or another—their own government is a feature of every imperialist war since the start of World War I in August 1914.

It was precisely this issue that split the global socialist movement in 1914. It was a division of historical proportion, a split that never healed and in fact led to the formal division of the movement into two world organizations.

BASEL CONGRESS RESOLUTION OF 1912

In 1912, two years prior to the onset of WWI, the international socialist movement convened a world congress in Basel, Switzerland. The Basel Congress, as it is historically known, passed a famous resolution vowing that should a war break out between the various imperialist countries the socialists would work against "their own" government's war effort, preferring its defeat and resisting the pressure to accommodate to the nationalist war fever that accompanies all such wars.

At that time, the worldwide socialist movement anticipated a new imperialist war was in the offing—just as we know, with absolute certainty, that U.S. imperialism is embarked on endless and

Lenin's concept of revolutionary defeatism during WWI is still a road map for fighting imperialism today.

repeated wars and interventions against all governments that seek to retain even nominal political and economic independence.

In 1912, the socialist delegates meeting in Basel pledged that it was the "duty of the working classes and their parliamentary representatives ... to exert every effort in order to prevent the outbreak of the war." Should the war break out anyway, the socialists agreed to an international strategy where each party would "utilize the economic and political crisis created by the war to hasten the downfall of capitalist class rule." This was the essence of a strategy that became known as revolutionary defeatism.

When the war broke out in August 1914, however, nearly every socialist party capitulated and found one reason or another to accommodate itself to the reactionary political climate created by the media and government. Demonization of the "enemy" was the propaganda method that captured the hearts and minds of big parts of the population, especially at the outset of the war.

A big part of the socialist movement openly and fully supported the war efforts of their own government. This was the right wing of the socialist movement but they were united, even though they had political differences, with a centrist wing of socialism. The centrists were "anti-war" in a general way and "exposed" the motives or some of the motives of their own imperialist government's war plans but they maintained unity with the right-wing socialists and refused to pursue the "subversive" strategy of the Basel Congress resolution.

The split in the international socialist movement put the right-wing and centrist socialists in one camp and it was they who continued to lead the Socialist International, also known as the 2nd International.

COMMUNIST INTERNATIONAL
AND THE LEGACY OF THE BASEL CONGRESS

The left-wing socialists declared that these organizations were "socialists in word but imperialists in deed" and they split and formed a new international body in 1918 that formally declared itself the Communist International (aka, Comintern) or the 3rd International.

The left-wing revolutionaries who had been isolated, hounded and prosecuted at the start of WWI because of their steadfast implementation of the Basel Congress resolution eventually became the leaders of anti-war revolutions that swept Russia, Germany, Hungary and other European countries in 1917-1920. Only in the Russian Revolution did the left-wing forces take and retain state power. The other revolutions were eventually smashed. Many of the right-wing socialists in the 2nd International became full partners with the police and army in the murder and jailing of real revolutionaries of the 3rd International.

When the Communist International was formed in 1918 it sought to reorganize the left-wing socialists of the world and based its political program and orientation on the critical lessons learned from the experience of WWI. It codified an anti-war orientation rooted in the concept of revolutionary defeatism and international solidarity against colonialism and imperialism.

In 1943, the Soviet leadership disbanded the Comintern, which had been founded as an instrument for global revolution and thus was thoroughly reviled and demonized by the western media and western governments, as part of an effort to create "good will" with the United States and Britain.

In the midst of WWII, Stalin was hoping that the dissolution of the 3rd International would be sufficiently appreciated by the Soviet's Western wartime allies (i.e. the United States and Britain) so as to convince them that their wartime alliance could morph into a period of ongoing peaceful and normalized relations following the war. The Soviet leadership, having lost 27 million people and the vast majority of its economic infrastructure in the effort to defeat Nazism, sought a period of peace with imperialism, or least a respite from war. However, this hope was dashed by the United States when it launched what was called the Cold War, by dropping atomic bombs on Japan in August 1945 and threatening the USSR with nuclear annihilation soon after the war ended.

SOCIAL IMPERIALISM IN A NEW ERA

The 2nd International continues today. Ironically, but not coincidentally, the same 2nd International-affiliated party of "socialists" controls the government of France today. On August 27, 2012 the French "socialists" called for the Syrian armed opposition forces to form a provisional government so that it could be recognized as the "legitimate government" by France and begin receiving additional funds, weapons and diplomatic authority. This leopard can decide to give itself a new "socialist" name but it retains all the old colonial spots that make it recognizable as a beast of prey.

As President, the "socialist" Hollande is the caretaker of the interests of French imperialism in the Middle East. Working with the Pentagon, the CIA and NATO, they are pursuing a policy of sending arms and finances to the Syrian "revolutionaries" to overthrow the Syrian government. The French capitalists, who were the colonial enslavers of Syria, have never fully reconciled to the reality of an independent government in Syria. Are they motivated now to overthrow the regime because they are troubled by the absence of democracy in Syria? To ask the question answers it.

The phenomena of some sections of the socialist movement supporting or accommodating to their own imperialist government's war propaganda and rejecting the revolutionary position expressed in the Basel Congress resolution has continued during the entire century of imperialist war that has followed. However, there has been a significant change in its application and effect.

The most notable difference lies in the nature of imperialist war itself.

The armies facing each other in August 1914 were from the respective major imperialist countries and empires. Each side had the capacity to invade, shell, bomb and impose heavy losses on its opponents. WWI was an inter-imperialist conflict.

For the socialists in Germany, France, Russia and elsewhere, adherence to the Basel Congress resolution took a great deal of courage. Pursuing a policy of revolutionary defeatism meant that these parties would be accused of being traitors, supporters of an enemy that could inflict huge losses on their own populations. Those revolutionaries who adhered to the Basel Resolution were sent to prison or worse.

Today's imperialist wars are one-sided affairs. They are waged by the imperialist countries against formerly colonized countries whose governments—whether they are socialist or bourgeois nationalist regimes—developed on an independent basis rather than functioned as clients or puppets of imperialism.

At least in 1914 at the start of WWI, when enemy armies were threatening each other's homelands, the socialists could argue that public pressure was too unbearable not to bend to the demonization campaign waged by their government against its enemies. For a Russian socialist, for instance, to argue on the basis of the Basel Congress resolution that the "defeat of their own ruling class" was preferable to its victory even when German armies loomed on the horizon took immense tenacity and steadfastness to the internationalist line.

How different is it today when "socialists" in the United States cannot rise to politically defend the independent Libyan government as it faced military annihilation by NATO bombers in league with the rag-tag militias of so-called revolutionaries? General statements issued against imperialism and NATO, that always denounce NATO's target in Libya as well, do not constitute an example of socialist internationalism. Rather they represent a form of centrism allowing the same "socialists" to effectively accommodate to the anti-Qadaffi demonization campaign created by imperialism's war propaganda while professing their earnest opposition to the war itself. Again, an expression of dilettantism taken to a new level!

Neither Iraq nor Libya for instance could send armies to invade the United States. They could not send fighter aircraft across the seas to bomb U.S. cities. This was not a war like WWI. All the bleeding was done on one side. There were zero American casualties in the war against Libya. It was actually more like a high-tech massacre than a war. If, during the conflict, U.S. cities were actually being bombed by Qadaffi's air force as Libyan cities were being bombed by the U.S. Air Force, these same "socialists" would have been outright supporting the "democratic" fatherland against the Libyan "dictatorship."

Today's wars resemble the old colonial wars and expeditions of the 19th century. The home population—with the exception of the soldiers in the colonial army—was shielded from the horrors of the war and its awful consequences for civilian life.

Iraq's army or the Libyan military could never have actually waged a mutual war against those who waged war against them. If they could have, any socialist in the United States or Britain who promoted a genuine anti-war position based on the Basel Congress resolution during the Iraq and Libya wars would not only have been branded an apologist (which is the preferred label used by both the imperialist media and the ISO for organizations like the PSL) for Saddam Hussein or Mummar Qadaffi, but would have been arrested and imprisoned as well.

The wars waged today by the Pentagon and NATO are not inter-imperialist conflicts waged to re-divide colonial possessions. They aim at rolling back or smashing the independent governments that came to power through the worldwide struggle against colonialism and for national liberation that became the hallmark of the post-WWII era.

The existence of a strong Soviet Union and the alliance of socialist bloc nations after WWII created a counterweight to imperialism that provided military, economic and diplomatic support for the newly independent governments in the formerly colonized territories of the world.

The capitalist counterrevolutions of 1989-1991 in the Soviet Union, East Germany, Czechoslovakia and the other socialist bloc nations removed this counterweight and ushered in a new era of imperialist aggression against all independent governments in the former colonies and semi-colonies. Not coincidentally the ISO and other "socialist" groups who champion the overthrow of the Syrian government today hailed the counterrevolutions in the Soviet Union and socialist bloc governments as they unfolded. Like the imperialist governments and media they hailed the anti-communist counterrevolutions as a victory for democracy and freedom.

THE REORIENTATION OF U.S. FOREIGN POLICY

From the very moment the United States succeeded the weakened British Empire as the dominant force in the global system of monopoly capitalism at the end of WWII, its foreign policy has been driven by four central priorities: 1) the subversion, containment and overthrow of the USSR and all of the governments of the socialist bloc nations; 2) the destruction of leftist and communist working-class movements in Europe, Latin America, Asia, the Middle East and Africa; 3) the annihilation of the national liberation movements in the formerly colonized and semi-colonized world and; 4) the establishment of global military hegemony through the placement of a vast worldwide network of U.S. military bases and the deployment of the most advanced nuclear and conventional weapons, a deployment far exceeding that of all the other imperialist nations combined.

U.S. foreign policy went through a reorientation following the epoch-shaping overthrow in 1989-1991 of the socialist governments of the USSR and its allied governments in Eastern and Central Europe.

For the past twenty-three years, the thrust of U.S. foreign policy has focused on the destruction of the independent states that emerged in the formerly colonized world which had managed to sustain their independent status from Western imperialism as a consequence of their economic and military ties to the USSR and the socialist bloc. This foreign policy thrust was particularly, although not exclusively, focused on the destruction of independent governments in Middle East where two thirds of the world's oil reserves are located.

As long as the Soviet Union existed, U.S. imperialism sought to manage and contain rather than destroy the non-communist independent, bourgeois nationalist governments in the Arab world. In fact, it preferred them compared to more anti-imperialist alternative movements that competed for influence in the oil-rich region. The

CIA and the Pentagon worked with some of these same forces, with the Ba'athist government in Iraq for instance, to crush the very considerable communist movement that was far larger than the Ba'athist Party at the time of the 1958 revolution.

The United States, however, never considered the Ba'athist government a purely puppet force as was the case in Saudi Arabia or Kuwait. In 1964, the Iraqi government announced its intention to create the Iraq National Oil Company and complete a nationalization of the vast oil resources that had been previously under the control of western imperialist corporations. In 1967, Iraq and the USSR signed the Iraq-Soviet Protocol which committed the Soviet Union to give technical and financial assistance to Iraq's national oil company thus allowing it to break free from the control of western oil giants. The country used the oil revenues to carry out huge social development programs that modernized Iraq, providing electrification, massive irrigation projects, free health care and free education.

When Mikhail Gorbachev became the General Secretary of the Communist Party of Soviet Union in 1985 he commenced a radical restructuring of Soviet foreign policy as well as the Soviet economic system.

In an effort to achieve a far-reaching accommodation with the United States and the dominant powers of Western Europe, his foreign policy signaled the imperialists that the Soviet government was willing to drop its traditional allies in Eastern and Central Europe and in the formerly colonized world.

Leading anti-communist right-wing capitalist politicians in the west like Margaret Thatcher and Ronald Reagan began a nearly open embrace of Gorbachev. Unlike any previous Soviet leader, he was the subject of immense flattery and praise by the western media. A new opportunity had suddenly presented itself to western imperialism. Immediately, the CIA accelerated its support for "revolutionaries" who sought to overthrow the socialist bloc governments in Europe while the Pentagon reorganized its Middle East war strategy in 1988 to target Iraq, which until then was considered an important ally of the USSR in the region.

By 1991, Iraq was devastated by bombing and economic sanctions from which it has never recovered. By 1991, all the socialist bloc governments of Europe were overthrown by imperialist backed counterrevolutions. Only Yugoslavia held out. But Germany, France and Britain began arming and financing various nationalist armies in Croatia, Bosnia and Kosovo and the dismemberment of multi-national Yugoslavia was well on its way. The 1995 NATO bombing of Bosnia led to the further dismemberment of Yugoslavia and the stationing of NATO troops in the partitioned section of the country. In 1999, the NATO powers conducted an unprovoked bombing war against the remnants of what remained of Yugoslavia. The prize was Kosovo. After the U.S. and NATO dropped 23,000 bombs and missiles on Serbia and the remaining parts of Yugoslavia and threatening a ground invasion in June 1999, the Milosevic government of Yugoslavia allowed NATO forces to occupy Kosovo.

The former socialist bloc countries in Eastern and Central Europe have now been largely incorporated into NATO either with formal membership or as adjuncts. The former Soviet Republics of Latvia, Lithuania and Estonia are members of NATO. The Ukraine has been incorporated into a strategic partnership with NATO. This huge former Soviet Republic sent troops to fight in Afghanistan as part of the NATO occupation force. Likewise, U.S. military bases have moved into some of the non-Russian Republics of the former Soviet Union including, Georgia and Azerbaijan in the Caucasus as well as Uzbeki-stan, Tadjikistan and Kyrgyzstan in Central Asia.

In the oil-rich Middle East, U.S. and NATO powers have, since the counterrevolutionary wave of 1989-1991, sought to weaken, subvert and then overthrow the post-colonial governments that used the existence of the Soviet Union and the socialist bloc as a means of protecting their independence. One after another has been targeted for overthrow.

Following the U.S. invasion of Iraq in 2003, Gaddafi's government in Libya saw the handwriting on the wall and sought its own accommodation with the West. It adopted a set of neoliberal policies and invited major western oil companies to set up business again, once sanctions had been lifted by Britain and the United States. As the Wikileaks cables of 2009 show, the United States was grumbling about Qaddafi's "economic nationalism" but still happy to compete with European powers for a piece of Libya's vast oil wealth.

The mass protest in Libya's oil-rich eastern province of Beng-hazi in March 2011, however, became ample basis for U.S. and NATO forces to seize the moment and use the anti-Qaddafi opposition as the premise for the full scale bombing of the country. They gave their mission a noble sounding cause, to "protect civilians," but then proceeded to drop thousands of bombs and missiles right up until the capture and murder of Qaddafi.

Wherever socialist and independent bourgeois nationalist governments have been overthrown the imperialists have moved in to exercise dominant control or at least far-reaching influence using both military and economic instruments.

If the first three decades after WWII were witness to a wave of national liberation movements and the establishment of socialist and independent, radical nationalist governments; the last quarter century has been dominated by a reactionary and counterrevolutionary wave that has strengthened the position of imperialism in many parts of the planet from which it had been previously evicted.

This does not mean that U.S. imperialism's power is unlimited. In fact, it may well be in relative decline and is plagued by accumulating contradictions within the capitalist economic system as evidence by the sharp, worldwide economic crisis that began 2007. But these limitations do not alter the fact that the United States and NATO powers, who had been on the defensive in the face of the global revolutionary tide following WWII, are now decidedly on the offensive and have been so since the overthrow of the socialist bloc governments.

THE TASK OF REAL SOCIALISTS IN THE UNITED STATES

Every war waged today by the United States and the NATO powers is a class war. The foreign policy of NATO governments is based on the needs and global interests of their own bankers and corporate elites. Imperialism is a global system, and the United States government is the anchor and leading force.

Every military intervention, covert intelligence operation, foreign military base and military assistance project by the Pentagon and the CIA is designed to strengthen the control and domination of the U.S. capitalist class over the globe. U.S. foreign policy is based on the calculations of empire. The Athenian and Roman empires of antiquity were based on the interests of the old ruling classes. The American Empire is based on the interests of the modern ruling class—Wall Street bankers, mega-corporations and billionaires.

The working people of the United States are constantly asked to send their sons and daughters to fight for and use their tax dollars to finance the biggest war machine in history. The targeting of independent and non-imperialist governments is part of a global rollback against the achievements of the anti-colonial movements that limited the previously unfettered control of the planet by a handful of western capitalist governments. Every war and every act of aggression is cloaked in the rhetoric of a supposedly noble cause: "national defense" or "protecting civilians" or "against dictatorship" or "rogue nations."

Until people see the underlying class character of every imperialist war and every aspect of its foreign policy they will be susceptible to routine deception by their class enemies at home. The role of real socialists is to unmask and expose the class character of the wars and machinations of imperialism and make it clear that the victory of our own class enemy in its global military endeavors only strengthens oppression, at home as well as abroad. □

Appendix

Libya and the Western left

BY DAN GLAZEBROOK

This interview with Brian Becker, national director of the ANSWER Coalition (Act Now to Stop War and End Racism) was conducted by British journalist Dan Glazebrook, on August 21, 2012, and has appeared widely. It is reproduced here with edits solely for style.

I **MET** Brian Becker in the Florida Avenue offices of the ANSWER Coalition (Act Now to Stop War and End Racism) in Washington, D.C., just across the street from the famous Howard Theatre. This area, Brian explained, has long been the center of the capital's Black community, and was hit by what were called race riots—"basically white people killing Black people in the streets"—during the white supremacist upsurge that followed WWI. The theater itself was used to set up sniper perches by young Black men to defend the area.

It is a fitting venue for our meeting. The ANSWER Coalition has, since its formation over a decade ago, worked tirelessly to oppose the racist wars of aggression that characterize the foreign policy of both our countries. Unlike some of their colleagues in the movement, they are clear that these modern-day colonial wars take many forms, including sanctions, covert operations, proxy wars and propaganda wars—and that all of these should be exposed and confronted. Recent mobilizations around the build-up of hostilities towards Iran, for example, were organized around the slogan: 'No sanctions, no intervention, no assassinations.' "Sanctions are not an alternative to war," Brian told me, "Sanctions are an act of war."

Like the antiwar movement in Britain, ANSWER achieved their biggest mobilizations to date during the run-up to the war on Iraq; a poster on the wall of their offices shows a sea of protesters in Washington, D.C., during the half-million strong rally that took place here on January 18, 2003. ANSWER's demonstrations against the war on Libya were sadly nothing like as big. I began by asking Brian why this was so.

> "What we witnessed in the run-up to the Iraq war was something unique. The justification and pretext for the war by the war-makers—the Bush and Blair administrations—was so transparently false, they could make no credible case that it was an act of self-defense. So the historic pretext and justification for war—that it is a response to imminent or actual aggression—was missing. And Iraq was obviously a hobbled country—it had been bombed mercilessly in 1991, it had been hobbled by economic sanctions which took the lives of 8,000 Iraqis every month, it was weak, and it was encircled by military forces—so the idea that Saddam Hussein was planning to use weapons of mass destruction against Iraq's neighbors or anyone else was so transparently false that masses of people were stimulated into activity."

This activity, however, resulted, in the end, in demoralization:

> "The movement had been built around the slogan 'stop the war before it starts', and so once the war had started the movement decided that they had failed, because the war had started—despite their monumental efforts and protests."

This should have been no surprise, however:

> "Whenever the imperialist powers, at least in the last century, have gone on the march to war, no protest movement stops them. Protest movements maybe ultimately overthrow the defeated imperialists—as happened at the end of WWI—but they don't actually stop the war. There's no history of that."

Furthermore, Brian argues, there was a crucial difference between the war on Iraq and the war on Libya:

> "In the case of Libya, the British, the United States and the French never suggested they were sending massive troops to fight; in fact, they pledged from the beginning that they would not. The British, French and U.S. governments promised their own masses that all the bleeding would be done on the other side."

Combined with the virulent and hysterical propaganda war conducted against Gaddafi, this made it much more difficult to mobilize against this war:

> "In the lead up to any war, there is a demonization of the targeted country and the leader as the ultimate devil, justifying any act of aggression. And in this war, no British were going to die, no French, no Americans: only Libyans would die, only the devils would die. So there was, on the part of the peace movement, an accommodation to imperialist propaganda because it was easier to accommodate to imperialist propaganda than to fight against it."

This propaganda went way beyond the Libyan government, of course, as Brian explains:

> "Any sign of support for Gaddafi gave lie to their propaganda presentation that it was 'the people versus Gaddafi.' And it is clear that Gaddafi had a lot of support from black Libyans who considered Gaddafi's African-centric foreign policy to be positive. So the manifestations of support for Gaddafi, or the targeting of black people by the so-called revolutionaries because they supported Gaddafi, created a contradiction for U.S. propaganda."

This is when "Susan Rice, U.S. ambassador to the United Nations, started characterizing Gaddafi's supporters as alleged African mercenaries." Despite the fact that Amnesty International could not confirm a single case of these 'pro-Gaddafi mercenaries', the narrative took hold. "This was an attempt by the administration to evade responsibility for what was basically a lynch mob atmosphere against black people in Libya."

Yet again, Brian points out:

> "...it shows that there is an organic connection
> between racism and imperialism, between racism and
> counterrevolution. These are fundamental organic char-
> acteristics of the social beast."

Brian is scathing about those sections of the movement that failed to
stand firm against the propaganda onslaught that laid the ideological
groundwork for the destruction of Libya:

> "Under the conditions of an imperialist demonization
> for the purposes of mobilizing our populations for war,
> we have to steadfastly stand against it, and be willing to
> endure momentary isolation by our critics who say we are
> apologists for the demon when we expose the demonizers
> as imperialists. If you cannot pass that test, you cannot be
> a credible antiwar movement, because demonization now
> is fundamental as a run-up to all imperialist war."

Indeed, there are historical precedents for this type of capitulation to
war-frenzy:

> "Let us also remember from the history of our own
> socialist movement that in 1912 when all the socialist
> parties met in Basel and could see the war coming, they
> all pledged that if the war were to begin, they would not
> only oppose it, but adopt a thesis that said "better for the
> defeat of our own government than for its victory." Each
> socialist party pledged to oppose their own ruling classes
> and their own imperialist governments in the event of a
> war and to take advantage of the war to promote rev-
> olution. Yet once the war began in August 1914, with
> the exception of a few parties and small groups, all of
> those movements found a way to support their own
> government.
>
> "They fell in line. Why? I would say basically
> accommodation to public opinion generated by imperial-
> ism. Each country was able to demonize the enemy, and
> the socialists capitulated. What we saw in Libya was a
> similar betrayal, a real betrayal of principle and of inter-

nationalism. You can always say that the enemy has certain characteristic features that make the war justified or at least rationalize your own inactivity in opposing the war. So, in the case of Gaddafi and Libya, parts of the left and the peace movement said, well, Gaddafi's rule was dictatorial, or he was a bizarre leader, or there was a violation of human rights, or there was torture, echoing all the arguments of the imperialists. Absent social pressure, all of the socialists in their meetings can make militant speeches to each other, and say we can identify imperialist demonization as a phenomena and we will oppose it. But will you go out into the public arena, when the public has been trained by the imperialists to say if you oppose a war in Libya, then you are an apologist for Gaddafi, for the demon? If you are not just fighting conservatives, but mainstream public opinion that has been poisoned by demonization, you have to be strong. Much of the left's betrayal of internationalism was nothing other than an exercise in cowardice, in accommodating to public opinion, imperialist-generated public opinion, but cloaked and masked in left rhetoric and human rights rhetoric."

He goes on:

"It's also nauseating that as the imperialists prepared for war and they [the left betrayers of internationalism Ed.] echoed the same slogans as the war-makers, that once the imperialists actually started bombing, they could say, 'oh, but we are not for that. We are not for bombing. We are for the end of the dictatorship. We are for the overthrow of the movement by the so-called revolutionaries.' That's just the height of hypocrisy and left demagogy. Why would the imperialists think that the NTC in Libya was something other than a puppet of imperialism when it decided to give them uncritical support? I mean, were the imperialists so uninformed, so blind and so unable to figure things out in Libya that they took the wrong side?"

As the true face of the "Libyan rebels" becomes harder and harder to hide, and reports of their atrocities and racism even seeping out into the mainstream media, it becomes increasingly clear that it was, in fact, the 'pro-rebel left' that took the wrong side. So what does all this tell us about the state of the would-be revolutionary forces within countries like Britain and the United States?

> "To actually carry out a revolutionary transformation of society requires a great deal of steadfastness and courage. If you could not stand up on the Libya campaign, how could you stand up on even bigger problems? At least the socialists in WWI, when they capitulated, could always make the case for national defense. The German socialists argued, 'well the Russians will invade,' and the Russian Mensheviks made the case that 'well, our country is going to be overrun by German imperialism.' But nobody can say that Libya was about to invade the United States, or bomb our cities or bomb the cities of Britain and France. The social pressure on the left is much less than it was in 1914 when there was actual bleeding to be done on both sides and so I would say the betrayal on Libya is even more abject than the worse traitors during WWI."

This historical analogy gets me thinking about where the new round of warmongering is going to end up. Twice before in history, massive global capitalist crises have led to a period of sustained colonial wars culminating in full-scale world war. Is this where we are heading now?

> "I think it is fundamentally different today. Until WWII the main conflicts were between imperialists, over the division or re-division of the world, because the entire world had been divided into colonies or semi-colonies or spheres of influence. There was nothing left to grab except from each other, and so they went to war in WWI and WWII. The old colonial empires were crushed under the pressure of WWII and the struggles of the colonial and semi-colonial peoples to be free, and the character of war shifted. Instead of imperialists fighting each other they were fighting a global united

front against the prospect that the emerging anti-colonial struggles would enter into a strategic relationship with the USSR [Union of Soviet Socialist Republics—Ed.] and the socialist bloc countries. The imperialist powers now seriously confronted the prospect of an end not just to this or that colonial empire but to imperialist domination everywhere. They all had something in common, and because the United States emerged as the sole super-power within the camp of imperialism it could organize this imperialist united front, assigning its former enemies in the case of Germany and Japan, and its former allies Britain and France, the role of junior partners.

"So what we call the Cold War—but which was very hot in Korea, and very hot in Vietnam and in many other places—was an expression of that global class struggle, where the two class forces had states and had state power, and warred against each other.

"But after the collapse of Eastern Europe and the Soviet Union, the nature of war went through another metamorphosis. Starting at that moment, and con-sciously, the United States set about to destroy all of those regional powers that had independent, anti-colonial governments. And that is what we have witnessed in the last twenty years. Take the first Iraq war in 1991. Iraq had been a principal ally of the USSR; the USSR ten years earlier would have never allowed that war to have taken place. Yugoslavia, too, was an important regional power that was destroyed by U.S., British, French and German imperialism. They tore that country apart. You can always find struggles between peoples and ethnic conflicts, but absent the determination by the imperialist countries to destroy Yugoslavia, it would have remained intact.

"Then when the neoconservatives who were the extreme expression of this military strategy, took office in 2001 in the United States, they were determined to accelerate that process. Their strategy that had evolved in the heady period of the 1990s, was to destroy Iraq, destroy Iran, destroy North Korea, destroy Syria, destroy Hezbollah's influence in Southern Lebanon and have a new proxy government in Somalia—that was their plan.

"Today, the neoconservatives are no longer in power. But the Obama administration basically pursued the same policy of the neoconservatives with tactical differences. At first the Obama administration's strategic orientation was to rehabilitate the tattered image of the United States which had been so shredded by its failure in Iraq. He seemed to be shifting the orientation that the neoconservatives had, because it is not good for U.S. imperialism to be so hated as it had become; it is not good for any empire to be just universally reviled and hated by all of its subjects.

"But then the Arab Spring emerged as an arena for a strategic recalibration of imperialist strategy, and ironically allowed the Obama administration to shift back to the fundamental premise of the neoconservatives: that the independent governments of the Middle East could, in fact, be toppled. Of course, people have grievances, and the ethno-sectarian and political divides that exist within all of the former colonized states of the Middle East also mean that these states are vulnerable. They have fundamental weaknesses which can be exacerbated by outside intervention, just as Yugoslavia's political organization as a multinational republic had a fundamental and foundational vulnerability. This vulnerability had not been exercising a dominant impact on Yugoslavia's political trajectory, but by virtue of imperialist intervention those fundamental weaknesses can be exacerbated once the regime becomes a target.

"So how could it be that Obama could adopt the strategic orientation of regime change against all these independent governments, which was the premise of the neoconservative position? The only explanation could be that the neoconservatives and the liberals within the camp of imperialism actually share identical objectives."

If these objectives include the destruction of independent regional powers, does this logic not also point in the direction of war against China and Russia?

"There is something about imperialism in this stage of its development where there is an organic drive towards counterrevolution against any political force that has emerged from the anti-colonial movements; because that indicates that there is a social force that can have independent authority over labor, land and resources. It is just like in the labor movement in the United States, or in Britian and Europe: even when you have unions that are willing to go along with corporate capitalism and make deals, the corporate capitalists do not want to go along with them. If you give them a pound, they say thank you, now give me another pound. So Russia and China, even though they do not have a socialist or internationalist foreign policy, nevertheless constitute an obstacle to the designs of U.S. imperialism and its junior partners in the EU and NATO.

"We can this see in the case of Syria—which is the most important part of the world struggle at this moment—with Russia and China uniting at the United Nations and blocking the United States from using the United Nations as an instrument for intervention in Syria. What a tragedy for U.S. imperialism! Not because they care about human rights or democracy in Syria, but it shows that there exists in the world today forces that can blunt the offensive of imperialism.

"This is not the nineteenth century, and the fantasies of the neoconservatives were burnt up in the battlefields of Iraq by an insurgency that could not be defeated, and are being burnt up in the battlefields of Afghanistan by an insurgency that cannot be defeated. In the instance of Syria, we are again seeing the limits of imperial authority, of U.S. imperialist domination."

It is an upbeat note on which to end. But it is clear that the imperial powers will throw everything they have into the fight to achieve their objectives. Since I met with Brian, the violence against Syria has been massively stepped up, with open arming and funding of the most racist and sectarian groups in the region and constant provocations and threats against the government. The anti-war movement in the West will need to massively build its clarity, militancy, organizational capacity and willingness to confront power if it is not to meet the same fate as the Basel socialists. ANSWER is certainly aware of the enormity of the tasks ahead—and, so far, have risen admirably to the challenge. □

Manifesto of the International Socialist Congress at Basel

A**T** its congresses at Stuttgart and Copenhagen the International formulated for the proletariat of all countries these guiding principles for the struggle against war:

If a war threatens to break out, it is the duty of the working classes and their parliamentary representatives in the countries involved supported by the coordinating activity of the International Socialist Bureau to exert every effort in order to prevent the outbreak of war by the means they consider most effective, which naturally vary according to the sharpening of the class struggle and the sharpening of the general political situation.

In case war should break out anyway it is their duty to intervene in favor of its speedy termination and with all their powers to utilize the economic and political crisis created by the war to arouse the people and thereby to hasten the downfall of capitalist class rule.

More than ever, recent events have imposed upon the proletariat the duty of devoting the utmost force and energy to planned and concerted action. On the one hand, the universal craze for armaments has aggravated the high cost of living, thereby intensifying class antagonisms and creating in the working class an implacable spirit of revolt; the workers want to put a stop to this system of panic and waste. On the other hand, the incessantly recurring menace of war has a more and more inciting effect. The great European peoples are constantly on the point of being driven against one another, although these attempts are against humanity and reason cannot be justified by even the slightest pretext of being in the interest of the people.

If the Balkan crisis, which has already caused such terrible disasters, should spread further, it would become the most frightful danger to civilization and the proletariat. At the same time it would be the greatest outrage in all history because of the crying discrepancy between the immensity of the catastrophe and the insignificance of the interests involved.

It is with satisfaction that the Congress records the complete unanimity of the Socialist parties and of the trade unions of all countries in the war against war.

The proletarians of all countries have risen simultaneously in a struggle against imperialism; each section of the international has opposed the resistance of the proletariat to the government of its own country, and has mobilized the public opinion of its nation against all bellicose desires. Thus there resulted the grandiose cooperation of the workers of all countries which has already contributed a great deal toward saving the threatened peace of the world. The fear of the ruling class of a proletarian revolution as a result of a world war has proved to be an essential guarantee of peace.

The Congress therefore calls upon the Social-Democratic parties to continue their action by every means that seems appropriate to them. In this concerted action it assigns to each Socialist party its particular task.

The Social-Democratic parties of the Balkan peninsula have a difficult task. The Great Powers of Europe, by the systematic frustration of all reforms, have contributed to the creation of unbearable economic, national and political conditions in Turkey which necessarily had to lead to revolt and war. Against the exploitation of these conditions in the interest of the dynasties and the bourgeois classes, the Social-Democratic parties of the Balkans, with heroic courage, have raised the demand for a democratic federation. The Congress calls upon them to persevere in their admirable attitude; it expects that the Social-Democracy of the Balkans will do everything after the war to prevent the results of the Balkan War attained at the price of such terrible sacrifices from being misused for their own purposes by dynasties, by militarism, by the bourgeoisie of the Balkan states greedy for expansion. The Congress, however, calls upon the Socialists of the Balkans particularly to resist not only the renewal of the old enmities between Serbs, Bulgars, Rumanians, and Greeks, but also every violation of the Balkan peoples now in the opposite camp, the Turks and the Albanians. It is the duty of the Socialists of the Balkans, therefore, to fight against every violation of the rights of these people and to proclaim the fraternity of all Balkans peoples including the Albanians, the Turks, and the Rumanians, against the unleashed national chauvinism.

It is the duty of the Social-Democratic parties of Austria, Hungary, Croatia and Slavonia, Bosnia and Herzegovina to continue with all their power their effective action against an attack upon Serbia by the Danubian monarchy. It is their task to continue as in the past to oppose the plan of robbing Serbia of the results of the war by armed force, of transforming it into an Austrian colony, and of involving the peoples of Austria-Hungary proper and together with them all nations of Europe in the greatest dangers for the sake of dynastic interests. In the future the Social-Democratic parties of Austria-Hungary will also fight in order that those sections of the South-Slavic people ruled by the House of Hapsburg may obtain the right to govern themselves democratically within the boundaries of the Austro-Hungarian monarchy proper.

The Social-Democratic parties of Austria-Hungary as well as the Socialists of Italy must pay special attention to the Albanian question. The Congress recognizes the right of the Albanian people to autonomy but it protests against Albania, under the pretext of autonomy, becoming the victim of Austro-Hungarian and Italian ambitions for domination. The Congress sees in this not only a peril for Albania itself, but, in a short time, a menace to the peace between Austria-Hungary and Italy. Albania can lead a truly independent life only as an autonomous member of a democratic Balkan federation. The Congress therefore calls upon the Social-Democrats of Austria-Hungary and Italy to combat every attempt of their governments to envelop Albania in their sphere of influence and to continue their efforts to strengthen the peaceful relations between Austria-Hungary and Italy.

It is with great joy that the Congress greets the protest strikes of Russian workers as a guarantee that the proletariat of Russia and of Poland is beginning to recover from the blows dealt it by the czarist counterrevolution. The Congress sees in this the strongest guarantee against the criminal intrigues of czarism, which, after having drowned in blood the peoples of its own country, after having betrayed the Balkan peoples themselves innumerable times and surrendered them to their enemies, now vacillates between the fear of the consequences that a war would have upon it and the fear of the pressure of a nationalist movement which it has itself created. However, when czarism now tries to appear as the liberator of the Balkan nations, it is only to reconquer its hegemony in the Balkans in a bloody war under this hypocritical pretext. The Congress expects that the urban and rural proletariat of Russia, Finland, and Poland, which is growing in strength, will destroy this web of lies, will oppose every belligerent venture of czarism, will combat every design of czarism, whether upon Armenia or upon Constantinople, and will concentrate its whole force upon the renewal of the revolutionary struggle for emancipation from czarism. For czarism is the hope of all the reactionary powers of Europe, the most terrible enemy of the democracy of the peoples dominated by it; and the achievement of its destruction must be viewed as one of the foremost tasks of the entire International.

However, the most important task within the action of the International devolves upon the working class of Germany, France, and England. At this moment, it is the task of the workers of these countries to demand of their governments that they refuse any support either to Austria-Hungary or Russia, that they abstain from any intervention in the Balkan troubles and maintain absolute neutrality. A war between the three great leading civilized peoples on account of the Serbo-Austrian dispute over a port would be criminal insanity. The workers of Germany and France cannot concede that any obligation whatever to intervene in the Balkan conflict exists because of secret treaties.

However, on further development, should the military collapse of Turkey lead to the downfall of the Ottoman rule in Asia Minor, it would be the task of the Socialists of England, France, and Germany to resist with all their power the policy of conquest in Asia Minor, which would inevitably lead in a straight line to war. The Congress views as the greatest danger to the peace of Europe the artificially cultivated hostility between Great Britain and the German Empire. The Congress therefore greets the efforts of the working class of both countries to bridge this hostility. It considers the best means for this purpose to be the conclusion of an accord between Germany and England concerning the limitation of naval armaments and the abolition of the right of naval booty. The Congress calls upon the Socialists of England and Germany to continue their agitation for such an accord.

The overcoming of the antagonism between Germany on the one hand, and France and England on the other, would eliminate the greatest danger to the peace of the world, shake the power of czarism which exploits this antagonism, render an attack of Austria-Hungary upon Serbia impossible, and secure peace to the world. All the efforts of the International, therefore, are to be directed toward this goal.

The Congress records that the entire Socialist International is unanimous upon these principles of foreign policy. It calls upon the workers of all countries to oppose the power of the international solidarity of the proletariat to capitalist imperialism. It warns the ruling classes of all states not to increase by belligerent actions the misery of the masses brought on by the capitalist method of production. It emphatically demands peace. Let the governments remember that with the present condition of Europe and the mood of the working class, they cannot unleash a war without danger to themselves. Let them remember that the Franco-German War was followed by the revolutionary outbreak of the Commune, that the Russo-Japanese War set into motion the revolutionary energies of the peoples of the Russian Empire, that the competition in military and naval armaments gave the class conflicts in England and on the Continent an unheard-of sharpness, and unleashed an enormous wave of strikes. It would be insanity for the governments not to realize that the very idea of the monstrosity of a world war would inevitably call forth the indignation and the revolt of the working class. The proletarians consider it a crime to fire at each other for the profits of the capitalists, the ambitions of dynasties, or the greater glory of secret diplomatic treaties.

If the governments cut off every possibility of normal progress, and thereby drive the proletariat to desperate steps, they themselves will have to bear the entire responsibility for the consequences of the crisis brought about by them.

The International will redouble its efforts in order to prevent this crisis; it will raise its protest with increasing emphasis and make its propaganda more and more energetic and comprehensive. The Congress therefore commissions the International Socialist Bureau to follow events with much greater attentiveness and no matter what may happen to maintain and strengthen the bonds uniting the proletarian parties.

The proletariat is conscious of being at this moment the bearer of the entire future of humankind. The proletariat will exert all its energy to prevent the annihilation of the flower of all peoples, threatened by all the horrors of mass murder, starvation, and pestilence.

The Congress therefore appeals to you, proletarians and Socialists of all countries, to make your voices heard in this decisive hour! Proclaim your will in every form and in all places; raise your protest in the parliaments with all your force; unite in great mass demonstrations; use every means that the organization and the strength of the proletariat place at your disposal! See to it that the governments are constantly kept aware of the vigilance and passionate will for peace on the part of the proletariat! To the capitalist world of exploitation and mass murder, oppose in this way the proletarian world of peace and fraternity of peoples! □

Extraordinary International Socialist Congress at Basel,
November 24-25, 1912.
Vorwarts Publishers, Berlin, 1912, pp. 23-27.

What is the Party for Socialism and Liberation?

The Party for Socialism and Liberation is a working-class party of leaders and activists from many different struggles, founded to promote the movement for revolutionary change.

Capitalism—the system in which all wealth and power is held by a tiny group of billionaires and their state—is the source of the main problems confronting humanity today: war, poverty, exploitation, unemployment, racism, sexism, oppression of lesbian, gay, bi and trans people, environmental destruction, mass imprisonment, union busting and more.

We are fighting for socialism, a system where the wealth of society belongs to those who produce it—the workers—and is used in a planned and sustainable way for the benefit of all.

The PSL seeks to bring together leaders and organizers from the many struggles taking place across the country. The most crucial requirement for membership is the dedication to undertake this most important and most necessary of all tasks—building a new revolutionary workers party in the heart of world imperialism.

At the same time as we aim for revolution in this country, we stand in defense of existing workers' states, national liberation movements, and for workers and oppressed people around the world.

To join the Party for Socialism and Liberation, see the contacts page or visit www.PSLweb.org

CONTACT THE PARTY FOR SOCIALISM AND LIBERATION

NATIONAL OFFICES

San Francisco, CA
sf@pslweb.org
2969 Mission St., Suite 200
San Francisco, CA 94110
415-821-6171

Washington, DC
dc@pslweb.org
PO Box 26451
Washington, DC 20001
202-234-2828

BRANCHES

Albuquerque, NM
abq@pslweb.org
505-503-3067

Baltimore MD
baltimore@pslweb.org
443-731-6471

Boston, MA
boston@pslweb.org
857-334-5084

Chicago, IL
chicago@pslweb.org
773-920-7590

Long Beach, CA
lb@pslweb.org

Los Angeles, CA
la@pslweb.org
323-810-3380

Miami, FL
miami@pslweb.org
305-209-2503

New Haven, CT
ct@pslweb.org
203-416-8365

New Paltz, NY
np@pslweb.org

New York City, NY
nyc@pslweb.org
212-694-8762

Philadelphia, PA
philly@pslweb.org
267-281-3859

Pittsburgh, PA
pittsburgh@pslweb.org

Sacramento, CA
sac@pslweb.org

San Diego, CA
sandiego@pslweb.org

San Jose, CA
sanjose@pslweb.org
408-829-9507

Santa Cruz, CA
santacruz@pslweb.org

Seattle, WA
seattle@pslweb.org
206-367-3820

Syracuse, NY
syracuse@pslweb.org

for a complete listing visit PSLweb.org

Liberation

**NEWSPAPER OF
THE PARTY FOR SOCIALISM AND LIBERATION**

Subscribe!

Also visit

Liberation*news.org*

and

PSLweb.org

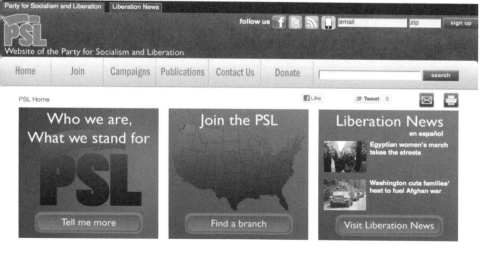

Program of the
Party for Socialism and Liberation

Socialism and Liberation in the United States
outlines the basic political and
ideological positions of the Party
for Socialism and Liberation, a
revolutionary Marxist party in the
United States. The book describes
the basis for a united, working-
class struggle against imperialism,
a system that imperils the lives
and livelihoods of the majority of
people in the United States and
across the globe. *Socialism and
Liberation in the United States*
envisions a socialist future based
upon principles of workers'
democracy, cooperation, equality,
solidarity and sustainability. It
argues that the workers who
produce all of society's wealth
should own and control it.

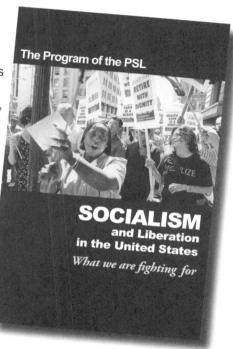

Available at
PSLprogram.org • PSLweb.org
and as e-books at
Amazon.com • BN.com

PSL
PUBLICATIONS

Paperback, 57 pages, $6.95.
November 2010
ISBN: 978-0-9841220-2-8
Library of Congress: 2010937412

PSL Publications
2969 Mission St. #200
San Francisco, CA 94110
books@PSLweb.org
(415) 821-6171

PALESTINE
Israel and the U.S. Empire
by Richard Becker

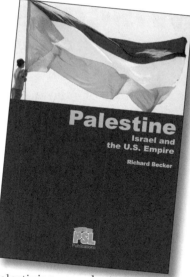

This book provides a sharp analysis of the struggle for Palestine—from the division of the Middle East by Western powers and the Zionist settler movement, to the founding of Israel and its role as a watchdog for U.S. interests, to present-day conflicts and the prospects for a just resolution. The narrative is firmly rooted in the politics of Palestinian liberation. Here is a necessary contribution to the heroic efforts of the Palestinian people to achieve justice in the face of seemingly insurmountable odds.

RICHARD BECKER is a writer and commentator on Middle East affairs. He has visited the Middle East on numerous occasions, contributed to books and videos on Iraq and Middle East affairs, and been a featured speaker across the country and around the world.

"Becker gives us the most focused and penetrating analysis we have of the real dynamics in the continuing persecution of the Palestinian people."
—**Ramsey Clark,** *former U.S. attorney general*

"This book is a clarion call to end the last vestiges of colonialism in the 21st century."
—**Imam Mahdi Bray,** *executive director, Muslim American Society Freedom*

"A must-read for anyone seeking to understand the Palestinian cause."
—**Samera Sood,** *executive board,*
Palestinian American Women's Association

"Becker foregrounds what others usually set aside: the integral role of U.S. imperialism, with the Zionist State as an essential partner."
—**Joel Kovel,** *author,* "Overcoming Zionism"

Paperback, 233 pages, illustrated, indexed. Price: $17.95
ISBN: 978-0-9841220-0-4, October 2009, PSL Publications

Available at PalestineBook.com and PSLweb.org
Also on Amazon

CHINA: REVOLUTION AND COUNTERREVOLUTION

China: Revolution and Counterrevolution features analysis of the Chinese Revolution, the present Chinese economy, the trend towards capitalist restoration and how socialists inside the United States can lend their support to the people of China. *China: Revolution and Counterrevolution* is a unique contribution to the left, using a Marxist analysis to identify political and social trends in China 30 years after the introduction of capitalist market reforms.

Sections include:
- **Overview: What do socialists defend in China today?**
- **China today**
- **China and socialism**
- **China's revolutionary legacy**
- **PSL Resolution on China**

This book is being used for study groups around the country. Consider ordering multiple copies and use it for collective study.

Order online at PSLWeb.org

Paperback, 193 pages, $14.95.
Reprinted January, 2012
ISBN: 978-0-9841220-4-2
Library of Congress: 2012930231

PSL Publications
2969 Mission St. #200
San Francisco, CA 94110
books@PSLweb.org
(415) 821-6171

The myth of democracy
———— and the ————
RULE OF THE BANKS

Author Richard Becker reveals that democracy in the United States is a myth, that it is the richest shareholders of the global banking conglomerates and other giant corporations that rule over the 99%. These banks were called "too big to fail" in 2008, but today have amassed even greater wealth through bailouts and mergers. Their greedy and predatory practices have resulted in millions unemployed and millions in foreclosure, while they amass record profits and pay out huge bonuses.

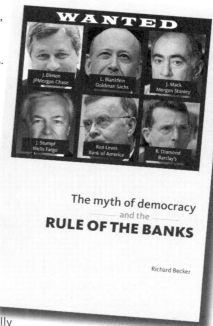

The case is made for seizing the banks. Not the money of individual depositors, but rather the accumulated super profits that have enabled them to become a critical lever of the modern economy and its political superstructure.

In their place could be a People's Bank, publicly owned with a democratically elected leadership. This new entity could then wield its power not for the rule of a tiny clique of bankers and other capitalists, but for the rule of the majority.

Available at PSLweb.org

PSL
PUBLICATIONS

Saddlestitched, 30 pages, $3.95.
September 2012
ISBN: 978-0-9841220-5-9
Library of Congress: 2012912890

PSL Publications
2969 Mission St. #200
San Francisco, CA 94110
books@PSLweb.org
(415) 821-6171